Life Cycles

Seed to Sunflower

Camilla de la Bédoyère

Sandy Creek
NEW YORK

Words in **bold** are explained in the glossary on page 22.

Sandy Creek
NEW YORK

An Imprint of Sterling Publishing
387 Park Avenue South
New York, NY 10016

Text © 2009 by QEB Publishing, Inc.
Illustrations © 2009 by QEB Publishing, Inc.

This 2013 edition published by Sandy Creek.

Editor: Angela Royston
Designer and Picture Researcher: Melissa Alaverdy

ISBN 978-1-4351-4710-2

Manufactured in China
Lot #:
10 9 8 7 6 5 4 3 2 1
04/13

Picture credits
(t=top, b=bottom, l=left, r=right, c=center, fc=front cover)

Dorling Kindersley 19t Peter Anderson

Ecoscene 13 Robert Pickett

Getty Images 5 Nigel Cattlin, 7t Nigel Cattlin, 9r Panoramic Images,
10c Nigel Cattlin, 11t Nigel Cattlin, 11b Nigel Cattlin, 12b Steve
Satushek, 14r Sabina Ruber

Photolibrary Group 1b Index Stock Imagery, 7r Gerhard Schulz,
10l Les Cunliffe, 15 Rob Crandall, 20 Gay Bumgarner, 21 Keith
Ringland, 23r Gerhard Schulz

Science Photo Library 8b TH Foto-Werbung, 9b Alan Sirulnikoff,
10t Steve Taylor

Shutterstock 1t Aga Rafi, 2r Eric Wong, 3t Gabrielle Ewart, 4l Amid,
6t Aga Rafi, 6–7 Pakhnyushcha, 8t Dabjola, 12t RTimages, 14l Sergiy
Goruppa, 14c Stocknadia, 16l Brandon Blinkenberg, 16–17 Javarman,
18–19 Vladimir Mucibabic, 22–23 Yuliyan Velchev, 24b Denise Kappa

Contents

What is a sunflower?   **4**

The story of a sunflower   **6**

Inside a seed   **8**

The first shoot   **10**

Sprouting and growing   **12**

The flower opens   **14**

Butterflies and bees   **16**

New seeds grow   **18**

Spreading the seeds   **20**

Glossary   **22**

Index   **23**

Notes for parents and teachers   **24**

What is a sunflower?

A sunflower is a type of plant. Most plants have **roots**, **stems**, and leaves.

Plants grow all over the world, except in the coldest and driest places.

⇐ Most sunflowers have golden-yellow petals.

Petal

Flower

Stems grow up
toward the light.
They have leaves
and flowers.

Roots hold the plant
in the soil, and they
soak up water.

Leaf

⇐ Plants need air, sunlight,
and water to grow.

Stem

Roots

The story of a sunflower

Sunflowers grow in yards and parks. Farmers also plant them in fields, so they can sell the seeds.

A seed is no bigger than your fingernail, but each seed can grow into a tall sunflower.

The story of how a seed grows into a plant is called a **life cycle**.

1

Seed

⇧ A sunflower has three stages in its life cycle.

2

Shoot

3

Flower

Inside a seed

A seed holds the beginnings of a new plant. It also contains food for the plant when it starts to grow.

A sunflower seed has a hard shell. It may be black, or black with cream stripes.

⇧ Seeds grow in the middle of the flower head.

⇐ If you open a sunflower seed, you can see the store of food inside.

8

This giant redwood is the largest tree in the world. It is 380 feet (115 meters) tall, but its seeds are tiny. Each seed is only a few millimeters long!

⇩ A redwood tree makes cones. Each cone holds many seeds.

The first shoot

When a sunflower seed is planted in soil and watered, it may begin to grow. This is called **germination**.

The seed's outer shell softens and splits open. A tiny root grows from the seed down into the soil.

⇧ The shoot grows bigger.

⇦ A shoot pushes through the soil.

⇦ The seeds are planted.

4

A few days later, a shoot begins to grow. The young plant is called a **seedling**.

⇧ The outer shell of the seed falls off.

5

⇨ Two small leaves open.

Sprouting and growing

Once the seedling has leaves, it makes its own food. The leaves use sunlight to make food from air and water.

The green leaves turn to face the sun. They collect as much sunlight as possible. Each leaf has tiny holes, which let air into the leaf.

⇨ All plants need water to make their own food and to grow.

The seedling's roots soak up water from the soil.

The seedling grows bigger every day. As it grows, new leaves appear.

⇨ A sunflower grows fastest in the first few weeks.

The flower opens

In the summertime, a green flower bud forms. The bud opens up into a big yellow sunflower.

The flower has a flat center. The center holds the male and female parts of the flower. They are needed to make more seeds.

14

⇧ First the green leaves open, and then the petals.

Stamen

Carpel

The male parts are called **stamens**.

The female parts are called **carpels**.

4

⇧ Yellow petals surround the flat center of the flower head.

Butterflies and bees

Bees, butterflies, and other **insects** are attracted to flowers. They see the bright petals, and smell their sweet **nectar**.

⇩ Nectar is full of sugar. It is food for butterflies.

Stamens are covered in a yellow powder called **pollen**. As insects sip the nectar, they are coated in pollen.

Insects carry pollen from one plant to the carpels of another plant.

⇩ Pollen sticks to the stiff hairs on a bee's legs.

Pollen

New seeds grow

Grains of pollen grow down into the carpels. They join with eggs inside the flower head. This is called **fertilization**.

When the eggs have been fertilized, they become new seeds. The rest of the flower is no longer needed, so the petals fall off.

⇨ Each sunflower head holds hundreds of seeds.

By the end of the summer, the plant looks old and tired, but it is still alive. It is growing lots of healthy seeds. The seeds swell and turn black.

⇨ The seeds are collected and used to make food for people and for pets.

Seed

Spreading the seeds

The seeds are **ripe** and full of food. They fall to the ground, or are eaten by birds.

Squirrels and mice also eat sunflower seeds. They climb up stems to reach the seeds, or collect them from the ground. They may drop the seeds, or bury them.

⇦ Birds crack open the seeds with their beaks.

↥ Squirrels hide seeds in the ground. They may come back and eat them later.

When spring comes, the seeds that are in good soil begin to germinate. They will grow into new plants, and the whole life cycle will begin again.

Glossary

Carpel
The female part of a flower. Each carpel contains an egg.

Fertilization
When a grain of pollen joins with the egg in a carpel.

Germination
When a seed begins to grow.

Insect
Small animal with six legs. Butterflies and bees are insects.

Life cycle
The story of how a living thing changes from birth to death and how it has young, or makes seeds that grow into new plants.

Nectar
A sugary liquid that flowers make to attract insects.

Pollen
Yellow dust that is made by the male parts of a flower.

Ripe
When a seed has finished growing and is ready to fall from the plant.

Root
The part of a plant that grows into the soil. It soaks up water and holds the plant in the soil.

Seedling
A young plant when it begins to grow from a seed.

Stamen
The male part of the flower. Each stamen contains pollen.

Stem
Part of the plant. Leaves and flowers grow from the stem.

Index

air 5, 12

bud 14

carpel 15, 17, 18, 22

egg 18, 22

fertilization 18, 22
flower 5, 7, 14–15, 16, 18, 22
flower head 8, 15, 18
food 8, 12, 16, 19, 20

germination 10, 21, 22
giant redwood 9
growth 8, 10, 11, 13, 21, 22

insects 16, 17, 22

leaves 4, 5, 11, 12, 13, 14, 22
life cycle 6–7, 21, 22

nectar 16, 17, 22

petals 4, 15, 16, 18
pollen 17, 18, 22

roots 4, 5, 10,
    13, 22

seed 6, 8–9,
    10, 14, 18,
    19, 20,
    21, 22
seedling 11, 12,
    13, 22
shoot 7, 10, 11
soil 5, 10, 13, 21, 22
stamen 15, 17, 22
stem 4, 5, 20, 22
sunlight 5, 12

water 5, 10, 12, 13, 22

Notes for parents and teachers

- Look through the book and talk about the pictures. Read the captions and talk about things that have not been mentioned in the text.

- Observing nature. Show children how to identify different plants that grow in the yard, park, or countryside. Look at different flowers and find the parts mentioned in this book, such as stems, leaves, flowers, and seeds.

- Seed activities. Sunflowers are easy to grow in the spring and summer. Place a seed in a pot of compost, water, and leave it in a sunny place. Water it regularly. When the seedling grows, observe how it leans toward the light. As you transfer the plant to the yard, you will be able to see its roots.

- Science at home. Find out how long it takes a seed to germinate and grow to full height. Keep a weekly record of the plant's growth—measure its height and count the number of leaves. Estimate how many seeds have grown in one sunflower head. Draw a sunflower life cycle with pictures of seeds, seedlings, and fully grown plants.

- Be prepared for questions about human life cycles. There are plenty of books for this age group that can help you to give age-appropriate explanations.

- Talking about a child's family helps them to link life processes, such as reproduction, to their own experience. Drawing simple family trees, looking at photo albums, and sharing family stories with grandparents are fun ways to engage young children.